D0274800

is book should be returned to any branch of the

BIG BU$INE$$

ASOS

Cath Senker

First published in 2014 by Wayland
Copyright © Wayland 2014

Wayland
338 Euston Road
London NW1 3BH

Wayland Australia
Level 17/207 Kent Street
Sydney, NSW 2000

All rights reserved.

Commissioning editor: Annabel Stones
Designer: LittleRedAnt (Anthony Hannant)
Picture researcher: Shelley Noronha

ISBN: 978 0 7502 8068 6
E-book ISBN: 978 0 7502 8551 3

Dewey categorisation: 338.7'61-dc23

Printed in China

10 9 8 7 6 5 4 3 2 1

Wayland is a division of Hachette Children's Books, an Hachette UK company.
www.hachette.co.uk

Lancashire Library Services	
30118129524595	
PETERS	J391SEN
£12.99	22-Aug-2014
ECL	

Picture acknowledgements: The author and publisher would like to thank the following
for allowing their pictures to be reproduced in this publication:
Cover: Asos image library; title page & p. 4: IanDagnall Computing/Alamy; p.5: Martin Karius/
REX; p.6: Ray Tang/REX; p.7: Alice Hepple/City AM/REX; p.8: Getty Images; p.9: WireImage/Getty;
p. 10: Andisheh Eslamboli/REX; p.11: UPPA/Photoshot; p.12: Bloomberg via Getty Images; p.13: Getty
Images; p.14: UIG via Getty Images; p.16: Getty Images; p.17: UPPA/Photoshot; p.18: Getty Images;
p.19: Shutterstock; p.20: Startraks Photo/REX; p.21: REX/Leandro Justen/BFANYC.com; p.22 Getty
Images; p.23: Kate Holt-SOKO; p.24: Shutterstock; p.25 & p. 32: Bloomberg via Getty Images;
p.26: Imaginechina/Corbis; p.27: Mark Sykes Moscow/Alamy.

The website addresses (URLs) included in this book were valid at the time of going to press.
However, it is possible that contents or addresses may have changed since the publication of this
book. No responsibility for any such changes can be accepted by either the author or the Publisher.

All brand names and product names used in this book are trademarks, registered trademarks, or trade names
of their respective holders. The Publisher is not associated with any product or vendor in this book.

Contents

ASOS was launched in 2000. Within a decade, it [beca]me one of the UK's largest online-only stores. By 2013, it [shipped] to 237 countries and around 1,500 new products were [added to the si]te each week. It was the most visited fashion website [... p]er day, by 18–34 year olds.

[As Seen On Screen'. As its [...] aimed at twenty-something [...] want to 'network, share [...] own style and of course [...] as a showcase for new styles, [...]g own-label collections and [glo]bal and local brands of [acc]essories for men and women [...] of affordable fashion as well as

catering to top style icons – ASOS is worn by supermodels and actors, too.

ASOS is based on a simple principle. To market established brands, it simply requires the production [...] and images from the companies that [...] them. People who sell from boutiques [...] photos of their goods, ASOS's website is [...] window to the world.

[...]y view the ASOS website [...]

This book looks at the rapid rise of ASOS from a website, set up by two businessmen in London, to an international company that achieved £1 billion of sales in 2013–14. It looks at the talented people and smart ideas that allowed ASOS to achieve this extraordinary success.

Singer Taylor Swift out and about in London, wearing a dress by ASOS

> In just nine years ASOS.com has gone from niche get-the-look website to massive Internet phenomenon.

Fashion magazine Grazia, 2009

Business Matters

$

Keeping the costs down

An online business like ASOS has advantages over high street shops because it can 'cut out the middle man'. It does not have the overheads of running shops, including rent, heating, lighting and wages for staff. All it needs is a website displaying all the goods on sale with details and images. Many items on ASOS are relatively cheap even though a large proportion are sourced in Europe. This is more expensive than buying clothing from China and the Far East, as many other retailers do. However, ASOS can sell the goods at reasonable prices because it is not paying to run stores.

As Seen on Screen

In 2000, Nick Robertson and Quentin Griffiths founded As Seen on Screen Ltd. It started as an online store for celebrity-linked household goods and other products. The idea was that viewers could source items they had spotted celebrities using on TV.

Nick Robertson (left), Lorri Penn and Quentin Griffiths in 2002 with some early ASOS products.

One of ASOS's first products was the pestle and mortar used by TV chef Jamie Oliver to crush herbs. It also sold a top that actress Jennifer Aniston had worn in the popular comedy Friends. The idea was good, but it was a difficult time to establish an online business. A large number of Internet companies that had set up when the Internet first developed in the mid-1990s were collapsing. ASOS's first year was tough; Robertson and Griffiths were forced to keep costs down. In 2001, they experienced a couple of months when it was hard to pay salaries.

An early shift in focus changed their fortunes. The first buyer Robertson and Griffiths employed to source goods to sell was Lorri Penn. She had been working for Arcadia, which owned clothes retailers such as Burton and Wallis. Penn recommended selling fashion. So ASOS now targeted 18 to 24 year olds who were keen to adopt the style of their favourite celebrity.

It sold copies of the most popular outfits worn by stars, such as models Kate Moss and Sienna Miller. ASOS sourced the clothes from small-scale designers. The shift to apparel proved popular. Selling an increasing range of items, by 2004 ASOS was highly profitable.

Quentin Griffiths' marketing knowledge was key to the development of ASOS.

Brains

Behind The Brand

Quentin Griffiths
Co-founder of ASOS

Quentin Griffiths and Nick Robertson came up with the idea for ASOS together. With a background in marketing and retail, Griffiths sat on the board of ASOS with responsibility for marketing. In the early days, Griffiths learnt from online sales giant Amazon about the need to know the customer: 'Understand your customer, who he/she is and give them what you think they want. You can find this out by surveying and hiring talented buyers who understand the customers.' ASOS adopted this policy, too. Griffiths found it satisfying identifying a retail idea in a new area and bringing it to life. In 2005, once ASOS was well-established, Griffiths left. He went on to set up Achica, an online members-only luxury lifestyle store.

ASOS on the rise

In December 2005, ASOS experienced a serious setback. A fire at the warehouse in Hemel Hempstead, Hertfordshire, forced the company to close for six weeks and resulted in a loss of £5.5 million. The fire destroyed all the stock waiting to be sent out for Christmas.

The company bounced back in 2006, with a big rise in online shopping, and ASOS's buying and advertising teams doubled. The following year, ASOS started up an own-label collection for men. To promote the company, it launched a fashion magazine, producing 400,000 copies per month for customers.

The dramatic warehouse fire – fortunately, no one was killed.

Business Matters

Going mobile

By 2010, people were accessing the Internet in different ways — on their computer, tablet or phone. ASOS was keen for customers to be able to access their sites on all devices, especially when on the move. ASOS Mobile was launched that year, and by 2011, ASOS was screen agnostic — this meant viewers could access its sites on any kind of screen. ASOS iPhone and iPad apps went live so people could shop from their mobile device.

In 2009, ASOS raised its game, adding a range of top designer labels and entering the world of high fashion. It also expanded its own-label brands, introducing ASOS Maternity and ASOS Black evening wear. The following year, ASOS offered free shipping on all UK orders. This was a major selling point because e-tailers commonly charged for delivery.

Developments in 2010 included the opening of ASOS Marketplace for the sale of second-hand clothes and start-up (new) fashion labels. The company took advantage of the huge appetite for vintage apparel and gave the opportunity for new designers to market their clothes widely.

The international market grew increasingly important. From 2010, ASOS established country-specific websites in key markets, first for France, Germany and the USA. In 2011, websites for Australia, Italy and Spain were added; by 2013 there were eight country-specific sites. The business was now so big that ASOS opened five international offices in 2012–13 to cope with the workload.

A party hosted by ASOS and fashion magazine Nylon in 2013.

Nick Robertson

Born in 1967, Nick Robertson is the great-grandson of Austin Reed, the founder of a well-known UK menswear chain. He grew up in Surrey; his father was a wealthy advertising manager. Robertson went to an expensive private school but he did badly in his A levels and left education at 18.

At 20, Robertson went into advertising, which helped him to understand consumer behaviour. First he worked at the advertising agency Young and Rubicam, moving in 1991 to media agency Carat. In 1996 he set up a product placement business with Quentin Griffiths, called Entertainment Marketing. This involved giving free props from advertisers to the producers of popular shows to encourage viewers to buy the products. For example, they provided Weetabix to appear in the TV soap EastEnders. Entertainment Marketing soon attracted big clients, including global companies Coca-Cola, Nextel, and Samsung.

Griffiths saw the potential to use the power of celebrity to sell products from popular TV programmes, and the idea for As Seen On Screen was born. With his wealthy background, Robertson was able to borrow £2.4 million from friends and family to set up the business in June 2000.

According to Nick Robertson, twenty-somethings spend 40 per cent of their fashion budget online.

Although head of a large company, Robertson does not overwork. He and his wife Jan have two children and he works reasonable hours so he can spend time with the family. In his free time, Robertson enjoys skiing and football and buying on ASOS. He says he's not motivated by money but rather by the 'pleasure of building and growing something.'

> " We've been growing at about 80 per cent a year. It has been a combination of lots of things – broadband taking off, the fact that we have so much product under one roof, a new way of doing something with a new generation. We have a lot of younger customers and when your Thursday, Friday, Saturday nights are what your life revolves around, what you're wearing is one of the most important things, and I don't see that changing. "

Nick Robertson, 2009

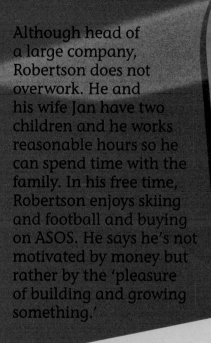

Nick Robertson, with his wife Jan, celebrates after receiving an OBE (award from the queen) for his successful business, 2011.

Twenty-somethings: working for ASOS

At first, ASOS was not seen as particularly fashionable. Yet by the early 2010s, it had a focus on high fashion, a website with continually updated style news and its own glossy monthly magazine. Seen as an attractive company, ASOS draws top-quality staff. In 2013, ASOS employed more than 1,300 people.

ASOS is a young company – the average age of staff is 27 or 28. Some work on its social media sites, putting material on Twitter and Instagram. Buyers choose garments to include in the thousands of clothing ranges on offer. Own-label designers visit the catwalks and travel abroad seeking ideas for their new creations.

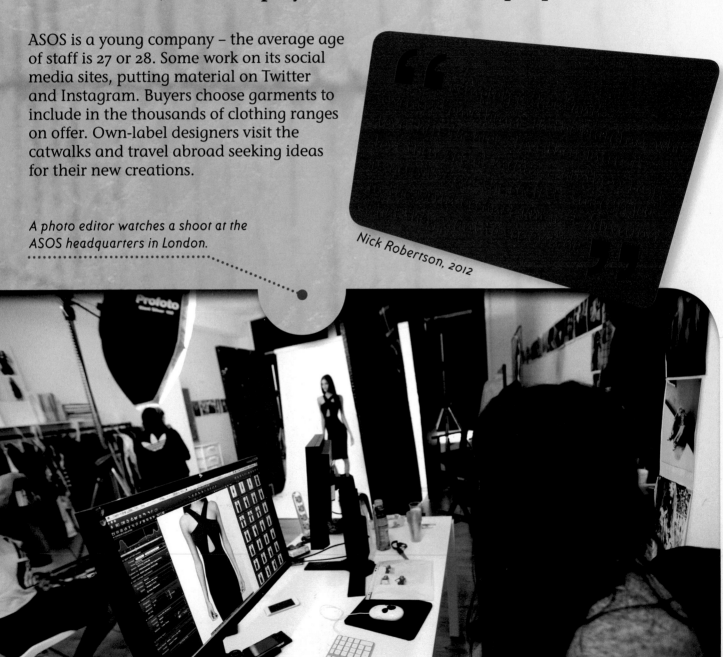

A photo editor watches a shoot at the ASOS headquarters in London.

Nick Robertson, 2012

Although there are lots of young employees, many of the senior managers who helped to develop ASOS from the beginning have gone. In 2013, three directors left, including Kate Bostock, who departed after just seven months as Director of Product. Bostock accused Robertson of pushing her out because she was 'too old' at 56. But Robertson claimed that it was important to employ people in their twenties because they are the target age of the customers. They source clothes and write news and information for people like them.

Kate Bostock accused Nick Robertson of being 'ageist' but he argued that she did not fit in at ASOS.

Business Matters

Perks of the job

Successful, expanding companies want to attract and keep bright young staff, and ensure they work hard. ASOS offers perks to create a pleasant working environment. During the summer, employees enjoy 'doss Fridays' — they can leave work at 3 p.m. On the last Friday of every month, free drinks are served in the chic canteen. Naturally, staff members receive a generous discount on ASOS goods, which they can purchase at work. ASOS pays extremely high salaries to top managers; Robertson argues that this is necessary to recruit and retain the best people.

Everything under one roof

ASOS's grand idea is to supply all its customers' clothing needs. As Robertson says, '[Our customer] is not loyal to anything, she has her favourites – some high street and some premium [high-priced], some eBay and some second-hand – why wouldn't we try to replicate [copy] that under one roof?'

ASOS certainly provides variety. It has 65,000 clothing ranges for men and women, including accessories. It stocks many popular global brands, such as American Apparel, Adidas, Esprit and Benetton. In 2012, it adjusted its collection to offer more products to people on a tight budget. The focus shifted from designer brands to affordable labels that people in their twenties were likely to be able to buy, including items from River Island, Warehouse, Oasis, and from 2013, New Look.

ASOS began selling River Island clothes in 2010.

Business Matters

Business efficiency

ASOS continually works to improve efficiency to bring new styles to market as quickly as possible. The company can respond fastest to new trends through its own-label ASOS brand because it controls the production process. To do this, it has streamlined the process from design to market, reducing the time each stage takes. ASOS also cut delivery times. In 2013, it trimmed the express delivery time by one day in 17 countries. Shortening the process from design, production to delivery enables ASOS to keep its prices down and remain competitive.

The company also sells many of its own brands, which account for around half of sales. Its own-label fashion is popular in the UK and internationally. Many celebrities have been spotted wearing it, including musicians Rhianna, Taylor Swift, Lana Del Ray and One Direction.

ASOS has many own-brand specialist lines, such as ASOS Maternity, ASOS Petite, ASOS Curve and ASOS Black x Puma sportswear.

ASOS Salon is a boutique line for women including vintage styles with embellishments such as sequins and trims.

With so much on sale, the ASOS site offers different ways to search: customers can shop by looking for the type of garment or accessory, or browse by brand or by store. They can indeed find all their clothing needs 'under one roof'.

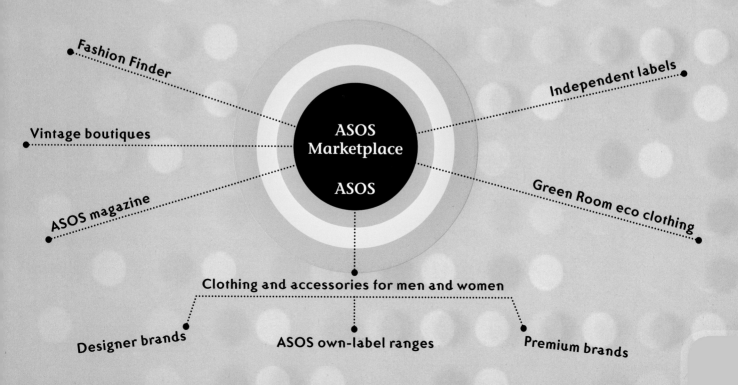

Fashion Finder

Independent labels

Vintage boutiques

ASOS Marketplace
ASOS

ASOS magazine

Green Room eco clothing

Clothing and accessories for men and women

Designer brands

ASOS own-label ranges

Premium brands

ASOS across the globe

International sales make up two-thirds of ASOS's business. For ASOS to sell successfully around the world, customers need to be able to log on wherever they are and see clothes that are in season and suit local tastes. ASOS has country-specific sites in its main markets, including Australia, France, Germany, Italy, Spain and the USA.

These websites are tailored to the individual country – they are not adapted versions of the UK site. The seasons are different across the world, so when you log in to the Australian site in December, you see summer garments. ASOS's approach has been extremely successful in Australia. Launched in 2011, it is the number-one apparel website there.

The websites for other countries, such as Spain and Italy, have increased market share in those countries too. But this doesn't happen automatically. When it sets up a website in a new country, ASOS has to raise awareness of its brand through a public relations (PR) agency. The agency reaches new customers mainly through online advertising. ASOS also has offices in the USA, Australia, France, Germany and China, with local staff who are best placed to target customers in their own countries.

Australian actress Isabel Lucas arrives at the launch of ASOS Australia in Sydney, 2011.

A big challenge for ASOS is organising speedy delivery of items. ASOS prides itself on offering free delivery worldwide, and in 2013 returns were free in the UK, France, Germany and the USA. The 'Follow My Parcel' feature allows people in its most important markets to track their deliveries in real time. In the USA and Australia, the largest markets outside the UK, returns are processed locally to save time and money.

> " We are in the right place at the right time. The Internet is growing very rapidly and online retail is growing at 30-40% and has done for the last three to four years. "
>
> Jon Kamaluddin, 2008

Brains

Behind The Brand

Jon Kamaluddin
International Director, 2009–13

Jon Kamaluddin had broad experience in accountancy and business when he started working for ASOS in 2004. In his early years with ASOS, he made sure that the rapidly growing business had no debt. After becoming international director, he helped to grow overseas sales from around 20 to around 60 per cent of total sales. Kamaluddin was responsible for improving shipping times, ensuring a smooth returns process and establishing country-specific websites.

Jon Kamaluddin always made sure ASOS's finances were healthy.

Marketplace and Fashion Finder

At ASOS Marketplace, people can buy and sell new, pre-owned and vintage fashion. Boutiques can sell their own label or vintage fashion directly to customers, and individuals can buy and sell garments. So how does this work?

Canadian fashion blogger Kiara Schwartz wearing an ASOS jacket, New York City. Street-style shots on ASOS inspire online shoppers.

Boutiques pay a monthly fee to ASOS to sell through its site and 20 per cent commission on each sale. For individuals, advertising products is free, but ASOS takes 9 per cent commission on sales. To showcase their items, sellers simply take photos of their garments and list them. When a buyer chooses an item, the seller receives an email and the money. ASOS Marketplace has proved profitable for the company.

ASOS's fashion updates are also successful – they inspire online shopping. The Fashion Finder section of the website shows the trends on the catwalk and on the street. It is packed with advice on what to wear for different occasions, from workwear to weddings. Inspiration from the catwalk trends and celebrity shots help users to style their own outfits. Boutiques have blogs on the site, and fans can follow particular boutiques or view their collections.

Business Matters

$

Buying safely online

When people buy from individuals online, they have to trust that they will receive the item promptly and in good condition. ASOS has built on the eBay and Amazon models to create a reliable service. Customer feedback is crucial; as soon as an item has shipped, the customer is asked to rate the service received. High ratings encourage others to buy from the seller. If there's a problem, the seller has to resolve it quickly to maintain their good reputation.

Many people join ASOS so they can upload their own photos and share their looks with others. Their images might show up-to-the-minute street style or an outfit they wore to a recent event. The clothes are tagged so that other people can browse on ASOS for the items they need for that look – for instance, the punk section has tartan clothing and garments with chains and spikes.

Anyone is free to upload their own style photos to Fashion Finder.

Connecting with customers

How many ways can a company stay in touch with you? ASOS connects with its customers through its website, social media, smartphone and tablet apps, and its monthly magazine. It provides all kinds of content – competitions, games, news, interviews and feature articles.

ASOS bloggers write about the latest trends in fashion and beauty. The 'Spotted' team roams the streets looking out for unique styles and snapping photos for the blog. Bloggers update the sites daily with photos and videos to keep them fresh. Other writers compile ASOS style news; in an effort to attract more male members, 'Medium Rare' provides updates and fashion advice especially for men.

Girl band Stooshe pose at the ASOS Music Lounge festival in Austin, Texas, USA, 2013.

Competitions are a popular way for e-tailers to engage their users. Contestants upload photos of their look to win prizes or vouchers for different brands. For example, a competition at the start of the academic year in 2013 encouraged students to send in their favourite college looks for a chance to win a camera.

The worlds of fashion and music are closely linked; musicians all develop an image based on their look. So music is another way to reach new customers. To this end, ASOS has immersed itself in the music scene: the 'Press Play' blog covers celebrity fashion and music. It has entered the world of live music too, organizing the ASOS Penthouse summer events in Las Vegas, Miami, San Francisco and Los Angeles, USA, and ASOS Music Lounge festivals in Austin, Texas.

The New York launch of the January 2013 issue of ASOS magazine, with cover girl Zosia Mamet from the TV series Girls.

Business Matters

Awards

These form an important strand of companies' PR strategy. They help to raise the company's profile, improve its reputation, encourage the staff and attract new talent to the business. It can be expensive to enter for awards, so companies target the most relevant and best-known ones. If they win, they make sure to spread the news as widely as possible — it can bring in new customers and lead to new business opportunities. ASOS has won a huge number of awards; in 2013, these included Best in the UK Customer Service Awards and Online Retailer of the Year.

Sustainable fashion

Would you prefer to buy clothing produced sustainably, without damage to people or the environment? Many people do! To promote sustainable fashion, in 2012 ASOS joined the Sustainable Clothing Action Plan (SCAP), which aims to reduce energy and water use in garment production. ASOS also works towards using lighter packaging and less ink on boxes to make them easier to recycle.

ASOS signposts sustainable items clearly on its website. It defines companies that develop fair trade, reduce poverty and preserve craft skills as helping people. Those that tackle climate change, preserve natural resources, reduce waste and care for animals have environmental benefits.

Michelle Obama visiting South Africa in 2011, wearing an ASOS Africa blouse.

The ASOS Green Room, launched in 2010, is devoted purely to eco fashion and beauty collections. To qualify for sale in the Green Room, an item must satisfy as least one of the principles of sustainable fashion: helping people or the environment. One collection is ASOS Africa. Since 2009, the SOKO workshop in Kenya, east Africa has manufactured clothing for ASOS Africa in a workshop that promotes local craft workers and sustainable business. It employs local people, mostly women, and pays them a fair wage. The Green Room is good for ASOS's business – although it forms a small part of overall sales, it helps to give the company a green image.

A SOKO tailor at work cutting out a pattern.

Brains

Behind The Brand

Jo Maiden
SOKO Kenya

Originally from London, Jo Maiden was involved in the Ethical Fashion Forum before moving to Kenya, where she set up SOKO with four tailors to produce clothing for ASOS Africa. By 2011 she had expanded the staff to 28. Jo tries to source as many of the fabrics locally as possible. All the tailors can already sew but she trains them to a high standard. Jo's biggest challenge has been to train tailors to produce garments consistently, such as a rack of dresses in different sizes but exactly the same in all other details, such as the position of the labels. SOKO also helps the community. Partnered with Ukunda Youth Polytechnic, it sponsors all the orphan students who study there, and it employs tailoring graduates.

Working towards ethical trading

ASOS has policies that require suppliers to meet 'or work towards meeting' ethical standards. What does this mean? To have high ethical standards, a company should be fair to employees, providing decent working conditions and reasonable wages.

The company holds discussions with suppliers in eastern Europe, China, Turkey and India, where pay is generally low, to encourage the raising of standards. Its 2013 commitments included setting up community-based projects to improve workers' welfare and tackle poor working conditions.

> To supply customers with high-quality fashion we need a supply chain that is responsive and reliable and which will work collaboratively with ASOS to achieve long-term, sustainable change.

Alice Strevens, 2013

Textile workers at a small factory in Delhi, India.

ASOS states that it does not allow anyone under the age of 16 to work for the company, so child labour should not be used. In 2011, ASOS signed a statement opposing the Sumangali scheme, a form of child labour in India in which young girls are contracted for three years to work extremely long hours for low pay in the garment industry.

Despite ASOS's policies on child labour, in poor countries, companies do not always stick to the rules. CEO Nick Robertson believes that it is better for people to have a job and an opportunity to rise out of poverty, even if the conditions are poor. However, ethical trade organizations believe all companies should meet ethical standards.

Ethical trade is discussed among ASOS employees at meetings.

Brains

Behind The Brand

Alice Strevens
ASOS Ethical Trade Manager

Strevens believes that ethical trade is good for suppliers as well as their workers. If they invest in the health and safety of their employees, their factories will run more efficiently. ASOS provides practical advice for suppliers through training sessions and site visits. These allow suppliers to meet and share ideas for good practice.

Strevens notes that it is relatively easy to improve health and safety, but it is harder to make changes to long working hours or improve wage rates. ASOS works to raise awareness of ethical issues among its buyers so that increasingly they choose to purchase from ethical suppliers.

ASOS aims for the top

CEO Nick Robertson believes that in the future, the Internet will have fewer but bigger sellers, and he hopes to develop ASOS's share of the market even further. To fuel growth, ASOS will invest massively in marketing.

ASOS plans to open more international offices and to become truly global by adapting to the market in each country. ASOS's ambitious target is to have websites that talk to 90 per cent of potential customers in their own language. A major move towards this goal was the launching of ASOS websites in Russia and China in 2013. ASOS aims to source enough fashion locally that consumers can choose to purchase clothes from their own country if they want to.

A young Chinese woman browses the Chinese ASOS website.

Business Matters

Marketing

ASOS spends huge sums on marketing, particularly online. It focuses on country-specific campaigns in its core markets, the UK, USA, Australia, France and Germany. It has also invested heavily in pay-per-click marketing, paying a search engine such as Google to place ASOS search results high up when users put in keywords related to its products. It pays a small fee to the search engine for each click on an ASOS advert. ASOS is very active in social-media marketing, posting daily updates with new ranges or sale items on Facebook and responding to hundreds of @mentions on Twitter, mostly from customers who are delighted with ASOS products.

The strategy to encourage fashion lovers to go to ASOS for all their fashion needs will continue: not just to shop, but also for inspiration and to communicate with other fashion lovers. ASOS aims to be available on all devices, at all times and to supply orders quickly while keeping prices down. In short, ASOS aims to be the 'number 1 fashion destination for 20-somethings globally'.

> ❝ More than just an online retailer, we want to be as synonymous [be the same] to fashion for twenty-somethings as Google is to search and Facebook is to social networking. ❞

ASOS website, 2013

ASOS's website for Russia was specifically adapted to suit the culture and has proved extremely successful.

Design your own ASOS product

To create a new product, it is helpful to put together a product development brief like the one below. This is a sample brief for Mini ASOS.

The SWOT analysis on the page opposite can help you to think about the strengths and weaknesses of your product, and the opportunities and threats presented. This helps you to see how practical your idea is before you think of investing in it.

Product Development Brief

Name of product: Mini ASOS

Design of logo: mini **ASOS**

The product explained (use 25 words or less):
Cute versions of ASOS own-brand T-shirts, jumpers, trousers, hoodies and sweatshirts scaled down for babies.

Target age of users: 0–2.

What is the product?: A range of babywear for fashion-conscious parents to buy for their little one.

Are there any similar products available?: None currently produced by ASOS.

What makes your product different?: It brings the convenience of shopping with ASOS to people buying baby clothes.

SWOT Analysis
(Strengths, Weaknesses, Opportunities and Threats)

Name of product you are assessing ...
Mini ASOS

The information below will help you assess the venture. By addressing all four areas, you can make your product stronger and more likely to be a success.

Questions to consider

Does your product do something unique?

What are its USPs? (unique selling points)

Strengths
Yes. There is no other ASOS range for this age group.

ASOS caters mostly to people in their twenties. As they grow a little older, they will start to have families but are likely to maintain brand loyalty to ASOS. It will be convenient for parents to shop for their infants when they order their own clothes.

Why wouldn't people buy this range?

Does it live up to the claims you make?

Weaknesses
There are many other popular baby ranges made by companies such as Gap and H&M.

ASOS sold a baby and children's range, Little ASOS, from 2008 to 2010, which it decided not to continue. The company would need to undertake market research to check that its customer base does now include significant numbers of parents.

Can the range be expanded in the future?

Will new markets emerge from this range?

Opportunities
Yes. If the baby range proves popular, it could be expanded to include childrenswear.

If the range proves successful in ASOS's core markets in the UK, USA, Australia, France and Germany, it could be extended to other countries.

Are there already too many fashion retailers making baby clothes in the market?

Is it the right time to launch the new range?

Are any of the weaknesses so bad that they might affect the success of the venture in the long term?

Threats
There may not be a market for another baby fashion collection. Parents may continue to buy ASOS fashions for themselves but shop elsewhere for their babies.

Little ASOS was withdrawn just a few years ago, so it might be too early to reintroduce another baby range.

None of the weaknesses are particularly bad. ASOS own-brands already have huge production and sales capacity so the risks of producing a small range to test the waters are not great.

Do you have the skills the company needs?
Try this quiz!

1) Your clothes from last summer are all too small. What do you do?

a) Wait for a parent or carer to buy you new clothes.

b) Suggest taking your old clothes to the charity shop and shopping for new outfits.

c) Pick out the old clothes that could be adapted to create new garments – your jeans are too small but you can cut them down to make a great pair of shorts.

2) You find out there's going to be a recycled fashion show at school. How do you get involved?

a) You bring along those horrible gloves your granny bought you. Well, that's recycling, isn't it?

b) You donate a bag of useful scraps of fabric, ribbons and buttons.

c) You embellish a boring plain T-shirt with fabric pens to liven it up and proudly bring it along.

3) At school, you're put into a group with some kids you don't really like. What is your next move?

a) You ask the teacher to move you, so you can be with your friends.

b) You just get on with the work, talking as little as possible.

c) You decide to give these kids a chance – you act friendly and in the end you get on with them fine.

4) Your teacher asks you to find out what people think about a leading company. How do you tackle the project?

a) You go to the company's website and get the information from there.

b) You look on the website and ask your family what they think.

c) With a parent or carer's help, you check out Facebook, Twitter and other social media to find out what people are saying about the company and draw some conclusions from your research.

5) Your teacher sets you a long, complicated maths problem. How do you cope?

a) To save time, you ask your older sister to do it.

b) You have a go but ask for some help when you get stuck.

c) You're really good at maths and you don't find the problem long or complicated!

Results

Mostly As: You don't seem to have developed an interest in fashion so far but this could change over the next few years. In the meantime, focus hard on your schoolwork and see if you can develop skills such as teamwork, which will be helpful for any career you choose.

Mostly Bs: You clearly have some interest in clothes and some useful research and teamwork skills. Keep working on these skills as well as your schoolwork, and a career at ASOS might be possible.

Mostly Cs: You already have a flair for fashion and some excellent teamwork, research and IT skills. If you develop all these skills and do well at school, maybe one day you could work for ASOS or a similar e-tailer!

Glossary

apparel clothing, when it is sold in stores

board a group of people who have power to make decisions and control a company

boutique a small store that sells fashionable clothes

brand a type of product made by a particular company

catwalk the long stage that models walk on during a fashion show

chain a group of shops owned by the same company

commission an amount of money that is paid to a person or company for selling goods

consumer a person who buys goods or uses services

contract to make a legal agreement with someone to work for you

country-specific website a website developed to be viewed in a particular country

designer label a collection of expensive clothes made by fashion designers

e-tailer a company that sells goods over the Internet

ethical to do with beliefs about what is right and wrong. In business, acting ethically usually means treating workers fairly and not harming the environment or wildlife

label a collection of clothes made by a particular company

marketing presenting, advertising and selling a company's products in the best possible way

overheads regular costs that you have when you are running a business or an organization, such as rent, electricity and wages

own-label a collection of clothes made by the company itself – for example, ASOS makes its own ranges of clothes

perks something you receive as well as your wages for doing a particular job

private school a school that receives no money from the government and where the education of the students is paid for by their parents

public relations (PR) the business of giving the public information about a particular company in order to create a good impression

ratings on the Internet, a measurement of how good a service is, according to its customers

recruit to find new people to join a company

retail the selling of goods to the public through stores or online

retailer a company that sells goods to the public

selling point a feature of something that makes people want to buy or use it.

shipping carrying goods from one place to another

sponsor a company that supports somebody by paying for their training or education

stock a supply of goods that is available for sale

streamlined to make a system work better, especially in a way that saves money

supply chain the series of processes involved in the production and supply of goods, from when they are first made until they are bought

sustainable involving the use of natural products and energy in a way that does not harm the environment

tag to add a link to a website – for example, ASOS members tag the items in the outfits they post on the site so that other members can click on the links to buy the products

vintage high-quality garments made in the past that are still in good condition and are resold

Index

BIG BU$INE$$

Contents of titles in this series:

ASOS
978 0 7502 8068 6

Heinz
978 0 7502 8066 2

Manchester United
978 0 7502 8067 9

Topshop
978 0 7502 8063 1

Virgin
978 0 7502 8065 5

YouTube
978 0 7502 8064 8

More titles in the Big Business series

978 0 7502 8041 9

978 0 7502 8202 4

978 0 7502 8200 0

978 0 7502 8203 1

978 0 7502 8201 7

978 0 7502 7090 8

978 0 7502 7088 5

978 0 7502 7089 2

978 0 7502 7091 5

WAYLAND

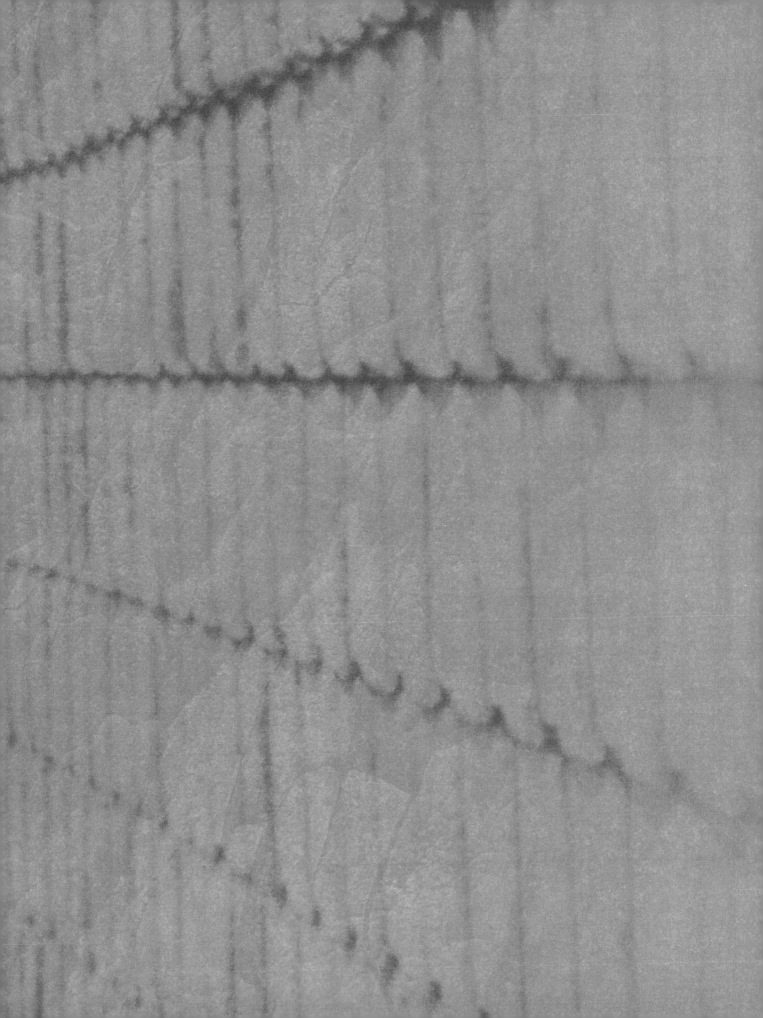